CURIOUS ANIMALS
OF THE PACIFIC NORTHWEST

CURIOUS ANIMALS
OF THE PACIFIC NORTHWEST

Volume I

Angela D. Goldsmith

Copyright © 2024 Angela D. Goldsmith

Wildwood View Garden Press

All rights reserved.

ISBN: 9798218366445

All rights reserved. No part of this book may be reproduced or transmitted in any form or by any means, electronic or mechanical, including photocopying, recording, or by any information storage and retrieval system, without permission in writing from the copyright owner.

To all the artists, known and unknown, who suffered for their craft and brought the rest of us immeasurable light.

"What heaven can be more real than to retain the spirit-world of childhood, tempered and balanced by knowledge and common-sense..."[1]

~Beatrix Potter

---

[1] Journal entry, from the National Trust collection, November 17, 1968

CONTENTS

Badger & Coyote, A Curious Friendship	1
Sierra Nevada Red Fox, A Secretive Vixen	19
Great Gray Owl, Silent Ghost	39
Acorn Woodpecker, Wide-Eyed Clown	57
Columbia White-Tailed Deer, Heart & Hind, Twice Shy	77
Western Gray Squirrel, Sciurus Griseus, A Haiku	97

FOREWORD

There is a lot packed into these short stories. My hope is that they will raise more questions in your mind. Citizen Science is the backbone of our knowledge base. So, do follow up with your own research and continue your journey, adding more knowledge to our collective wisdom.

While I wrote each of these stories based in a particular ecoregion of the states of Oregon and south Washington, the animals portrayed don't abide by our made-up divisions; they cross regions. Some live across the continent, even around the world. Some behaviors are distinct to each area, just like the language of our ubiquitous Corvids. Unfortunately, some species are only known to exist in a few small geographic regions, and there are too many, in one small space.

Most of the artists' portrayals of the species are based on my own trail camera photos, video and nature photography. For species that are rarely seen such as the Sierra Nevada Red Fox, trail cams and artists' imaginations are used based on available data.

All of the lyrical prose presented began as different styles of poetry. They have been adapted to book form in collaboration with the artists.

And most of all, data changes as our observations and interactions with the world change. All data has been verified to the best of the author's ability at the time of Wildwood View Garden's publication of the original chapbooks and their most recent iterations.

ACKNOWLEDGMENTS

I would like to recognize and thank all the organizations and others that have led me to this publication.

First and foremost, I bow to every one of the artists who have agreed to collaborate with me on this project. Your craft is indispensable to a beautiful world. I feel so privileged to be a part of the works in this book.

Also to:

University of Oregon Naturalist Program, for the opportunities to educate, engage, and collaborate with like-minded citizen scientists.

Cascadia Wild and Teri Lysak, for keeping me on the trail throughout the year.

Depave Portland and Arif Ilahi Kahn, who catalyzed my entry into the world of permaculture.

To the men who re-galvanized the sustainable agricultural movement first employed by the first peoples of all nations, [2]David Holmgren and the late Bill Mollison without whom my soil would be uncovered, dry and dead.

To my fellow indie authors at Northwest Independent Writers Association (NIWA). You've been an amazing group with which to work.

---

[2] The names of the principles of permaculture are from *David Holmgren's *Permaculture-Principles and Pathways Beyond Sustainability*.

INTRODUCTION

I believe that utilizing our human understanding of, and connection with, other species is paramount for the good of all life into the future.

From Aesop's Fables to Stephen Cosgrove's "Wheedle On The Needle" and others, I have had a fascination with fables since I was a child. They share with us society's concepts of behavior through the ethos of the species portrayed in these stories.

As a Certified Naturalist in the state of Oregon and long-time student and teacher of permaculture, I wanted to bring these two disciplines together and share my love of this region in which I have lived all my life, the Pacific Northwest. Here are stories about a conservation species (species of interest and/or concern) or two in each eco-region of the state. In each story in this volume, they exemplify six of the twelve permaculture principles in their behavior; behaviors that govern a way of sustainable life.

I turn these stories over to you, and I challenge you to find your place in them.

After all, we are Of Nature, not outside of it.

Best to you all,
Angela

Artist **Quin Sweetman** combines her passion for the outdoors with her love of expression. Inspired by the great Impressionists and Expressionists, she is drawn by the abstract shapes, the flow of line, the sweep of color, and energy in a broad and striking view. "I want to convey the unique energy of a subject, whether it be animal, human, landscape, building or action."

Badger & Coyote is Sweetman's first book illustration project. She is happy to pair her sketching ability with her friend's writing to bring to life another unique partnership. You can see more of her work at www.quinsweetman.com.

BADGER & COYOTE

A Curious Friendship

Artist Quineccoe J Sweetman

CURIOUS ANIMALS

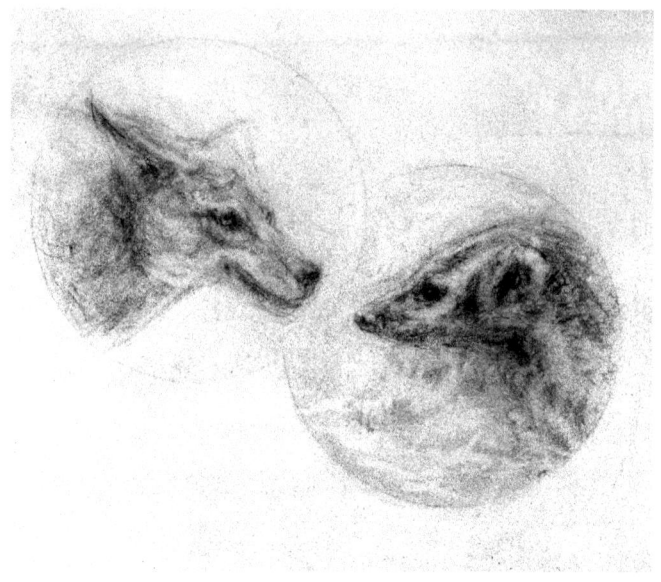

Today in another place, a place which you probably are not, a place that humans rarely see,

BADGER & COYOTE

a Badger and Coyote's partnership has come to be.

CURIOUS ANIMALS

This is the vast Columbia Plateau. Where mountains to the West rise out of the ground, like ice-cream cones filled upside down.

BADGER & COYOTE

Where hills to the East gently roll into a broad hazy sky; wave upon wave of ground.

CURIOUS ANIMALS

Somewhere out here in the bunch grasses,
Badger and Coyote hunt during Spring,
Summer and Fall.

BADGER & COYOTE

"What a curious friendship," I hear you say. "We think Badger is cranky and Coyote likes to play."

CURIOUS ANIMALS

These two have their special talents, and together they make a team. Badger has front paws with long curved digging claws.

BADGER & COYOTE

Coyote can dig at the Ground Squirrel's door, and he can run faster than a sunbeam.

CURIOUS ANIMALS

He watches and waits nearby, keeping his eye on all the exits. Badger digs at an entrance until she reaches her prey.

In a flash, the Ground Squirrel races out the other way. There is Coyote ready to pounce on his meal of the day.

CURIOUS ANIMALS

Sometimes they fail and that's alright; they will eat the next day. And sometimes they don't even share, and that's okay too;

because, if they keep hunting together,
they'll each help the other make do.

CURIOUS ANIMALS

Winter turns to Spring and there is melting snow. Then Spring turns to Summer and no animal wants to hide low.

BADGER & COYOTE

When Summer turns to Fall, Badger and
Coyote continue to hunt together
until the Winter winds start to blow.

CURIOUS ANIMALS

The Columbia Plateau is a majestic place to behold! Stand somewhere out there and take a moment to feel small and insignificant. Reground in your purpose.

Badger and Coyote have other friends here: Burrowing Owl, Bull Trout, Long-Billed Curlew, the Washington Ground Squirrel, and so many others.

Badger and Coyote demonstrate Permaculture Principle #10, Use and Value Diversity. This principle on the Columbia Plateau is especially important. It is a harsh environment. This pair's partnership was known by the First People long ago. Notably, they hunt together during all seasons but Winter. Despite the current challenges they face as humans have fragmented animal hunting grounds with fencing and replacement of native vegetation with cropland, they survive.

They use and value diversity in each other's ' talents through the changing seasons. A pack of Coyotes might not eat as well in this territory as the Badger and a solo Coyote friend. And certainly, a Badger alone may not do well either. They are different species with differing talents. They use them together to survive.

Artist **Jinnet Powel** has been sketching and dabbling in art since first picking up a stick of charcoal in her dad's studio. Painting for our local wildlife has been a passion since moving to Oregon in 2000. Biodiverse landscapes are healthy landscapes. You can follow her work at @Jkpowel on Instagram.

Sierra Nevada Red Fox

A Secretive Vixen

Artist Jinnet Powel

CURIOUS ANIMALS

Fantastic Mrs. Fox lives high up in the mountain snow.

She is called a "Sierra Nevada Red Fox", and her numbers are very, very low.

SIERRA NEVADA RED FOX

So, unlike her Red Fox cousins

who live almost everywhere in the world below.

CURIOUS ANIMALS

This fox is rare and so hard to find

that we don't exactly know what she is about.

SIERRA NEVADA RED FOX

Except, that she IS a fox, without a doubt.

She is a vixen of the first degree!

CURIOUS ANIMALS

Our Montane Fox has colors which change,
sometimes black, silver or red.

The seasons rearrange the fur on this
vixen's head

SIERRA NEVADA RED FOX

Her family has a cozy, secret and carefully chosen den,

where she keeps her playful kits, perfect just for them.

CURIOUS ANIMALS

When they are old enough to be out of the den to see,

they view their new wide world
and space to run free!

SIERRA NEVADA RED FOX

In the High Cascades with their big conifer trees,

and the shining Spring sun;

CURIOUS ANIMALS

while mom and dad hunt, the kits have fun.

They learn to fight during their play. Who is the stronger one?

SIERRA NEVADA RED FOX

Mrs. Vixen with tall ears and tilted head;

and pert, turned up nose….

CURIOUS ANIMALS

she can hear across the field,
a tiny mouse

in the deep Winter snows.

SIERRA NEVADA RED FOX

With her head turned North,

she waits in a huntress pose.

CURIOUS ANIMALS

When she hears movement, however small,

she pounces deep, balancing with her tail.

SIERRA NEVADA RED FOX

She rarely misses,

so her kits are guaranteed
a very necessary meal.

CURIOUS ANIMALS

The Cascades (East and West) are a beautiful, and mostly uninhabited place. Covered in large stands of Douglas Fir and other conifers above 4,000ft there are private meadows where the SNRF resides.

The Sierra Nevada Red Fox is currently only known to exist in a couple of very small pockets of their native Cascade Range. In the past decade or so, several have been seen on Mt. Hood via trail camera. Regionally isolated from others of their species in the Southern Oregon Cascades and the California Sierra Nevadas, they are in danger of extinction due to this isolation and their small numbers. In the past, hunted as an invasive species, they now have protection as a native and threatened species. Currently only 50 are believed to exist.

There are also continued threats to their montane meadow; the increase of young encroaching trees, the increasing temperatures, the competition with and being prey to coyotes. They are only the size of a large house cat!

The Sierra Nevada Red Fox and the Red Fox habitats are divided by elevation. At the time of this writing, a SNRF was seen via trail camera at a lower elevation than it was previously thought to traverse. Though a biological possibility for crossbreeding exists, it seems unlikely. High mountain snow appears critical to breeding and rearing for the SNRF.

Just as they are prey to the encroaching Coyote, the natural allowance of Wolves in the territory that prey on the Coyote would in turn assist the SNRF population. Simply put, they need more protections.

CURIOUS ANIMALS

"Great Gray Owl" is Quineccoe J. Sweetman's first official foray into watercolor, a very different medium than her traditional oils. She is enjoying how this medium brings out subtle color and evokes mystery of the subjects in this chapter.

GREAT GRAY OWL

A Silent Ghost

Artist Quineccoe J Sweetman

CURIOUS ANIMALS

The Great Gray Owl sits on the snag of a tree, at the edge of a high mountain forest.

GREAT GRAY OWL

Overlooking the meadows that spread like a sea, he patiently waits for a sound to reach him.
The faintest.

CURIOUS ANIMALS

This fluffiest of owls with a dinner-plate face,
and a look of surprise in his yellow eyes;

GREAT GRAY OWL

he is so very hard to find, so tough to place.
He is the most secretive of birds.
The stillest.

CURIOUS ANIMALS

He begins his hunt in the earliest hours of night,
moving his feathered head all around.

GREAT GRAY OWL

Launching from his look-out with his slow
wing-ed flight, very suddenly, he drops
straight down.
The lowest.

CURIOUS ANIMALS

Into the tall meadow grass, the raptor dives for his prey, using his uneven ears to catch the sound of his owlets' next meal.

GREAT GRAY OWL

In his beak it does sway, as he flies up and back into the trees.
The quietest.

CURIOUS ANIMALS

Somewhere out there on the forested mountain slopes, his mate sits near a borrowed nest.

GREAT GRAY OWL

Their white-feathered young filled with hope,
all looking to him with hungry eyes.
The hungriest.

CURIOUS ANIMALS

He now delivers fresh-caught meat.
From beak to beak it is passed.

GREAT GRAY OWL

Then with his ever slow wing-ed beat, his ghostly form disappears, into the thick blanket of fog.
The thickest.

CURIOUS ANIMALS

The Eastern slopes of the Cascade Range is a dry mixture of varying scenes from sagebrush country to alpine meadows. It is one of the most biologically diverse ecoregions in Oregon.

You will find Great Gray Owl in high mountain forests of Lodgepole Pine all the way to low mixed Oak Woodland. The family nests in amongst the trees, but hunts at the margins. Food is easiest to gain in an open montane meadow or a 2-4 year burn where the rodent prey have returned. They average 30" tall with a 5 ft wingspan and can hear a Vole at 100 yards, 2ft under the snow. This "Ghost of the Forest" is non-aggressive and hard to find.

Great Gray Owl has other friends here: Black-Backed Woodpecker, Caspian Tern,

Gray Wolf, Greater Sandhill Crane, Long-billed Curlew, Northern Goshawk, and many more!

The Great Gray Owl demonstrates Permaculture Principle #11, Uses Edges and Values the Marginal. This principle recognizes that most food sources are found around the edge whether forest-to-meadow or in the cultivated garden. With protection at their back and sun on their face, plants and animals grow and thrive here.

CURIOUS ANIMALS

GREAT GRAY OWL

Artist **Suzy Kitman** is a classically trained painter working in Portland, Oregon. Her work has been exhibited, published and included in private and public collections across the country. Suzy continues to teach painting. Please visit www.suzykitman.com to see examples of her work, for upcoming show information, classes and to learn more about commissions.

ACORN WOODPECKER

Wide-Eyed Clown

Artist Suzy Kiman

CURIOUS ANIMALS

Way up high, but not too high to see, there lives a

ACORN WOODPECKER

large family of birds,
Acorn Woodpeckers

CURIOUS ANIMALS

as content as can be,
spending their days pecking

ACORN WOODPECKER

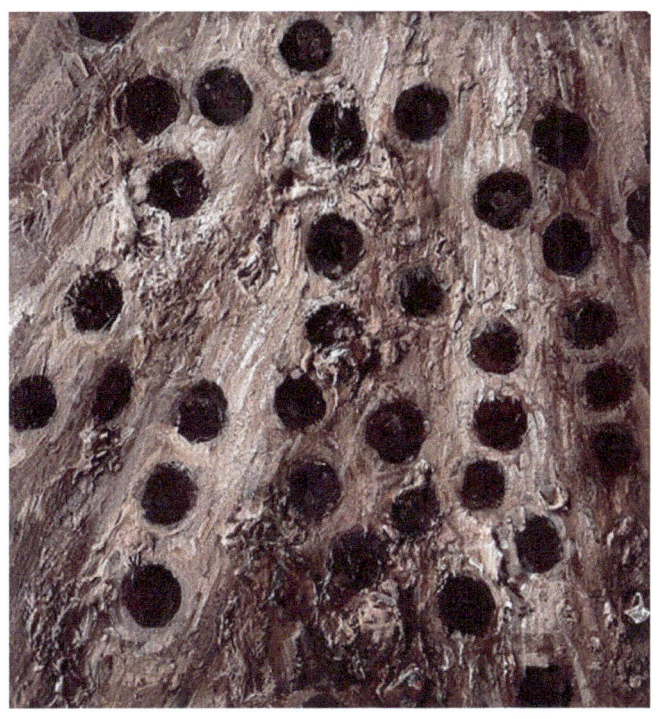

holes in the trunk of a
Giant Sequoia Tree.

CURIOUS ANIMALS

"So crazy! Why?" You ask.
"What could be at stake?"

ACORN WOODPECKER

Family's nutty stores
of snugly fitted acorns.

CURIOUS ANIMALS

Diligently they take
and hammer into holes,

ACORN WOODPECKER

lest the brazen Jay birds
and sneaky Gray Squirrels

CURIOUS ANIMALS

leave our bushel of birds
without their Winter food to partake.

ACORN WOODPECKER

With an arrow-like bent,
whir of their quick wings

CURIOUS ANIMALS

and bright, red-headed flash,
insects are their main thing.

ACORN WOODPECKER

Cousins, aunts and brothers
eat on the wing.

CURIOUS ANIMALS

But when the cold descends
on the Willamette Valley ground,
and the insects are asleep,

ACORN WOODPECKER

you hear a riot of woodpecker sound.
These "wide-eyed clowns."[3]

---

[3] Quoted from Cornell Lab of Ornithology

CURIOUS ANIMALS

The Willamette Valley is a lovely swathe of land between the Coastal and Cascade Mountain Ranges. As little as 2% and 7% of the once extensive Black and White Oak Trees still stand where farmland and small towns have taken over. But strategies to preserve and even plant anew have begun.

The Acorn Woodpecker is found as far north as Klickitat and Skamania Counties in Washington State. It is abundant the further south we go in Southern Oregon all the way to Mexico. Their granaries can be found in standing snags as well as conifer trees such as Sequoia and firs.

It's a regular party in a 300+ year old White Oak Tree! Townsend's Big-Eared Bat, Northern Red-Legged Frog, Western Painted

ACORN WOODPECKER

Turtle, Fender's Blue Butterfly, and others join our woodpecker in the valley.

Acorn Woodpecker demonstrates Permaculture Principle #3, Obtaining a Yield. While planning ahead for more permanent food sources, operating with an eye on long term nutrient solutions, one must eat more immediately.

Just like many of us animals, putting food by is a must for the off season, to stay alive. But you must eat while you are obtaining your yield, and so the Acorn Woodpecker needs as well. While they mostly survive on the insect populations in the woodland and the marshes along the rivers during Spring, Summer and Fall, they rely on the acorns and nuts for Winter fare.

CURIOUS ANIMALS

Acorn Woodpeckers live in large family groups. They have more than one mate. Anywhere from 2 to fifteen parents tend a single nest. One third of the population are helpers in the family and non-breeding. Some granary trees have more than 50,000 holes and take generations to create.[4]

---

[4] One wildlife biologist states, "I've never seen acorn woodpeckers hunt for insects on the wing like Lewis' woodpeckers. The acorn woodpeckers here (Columbia River Gorge area) pursue insects on the oaks and pines."

ACORN WOODPECKER

Artist **Leah Kohlenberg** is an acrylic artist that focuses on large scale, abstract flora & cityscapes. This project was her first small scale series; a challenge and delight. See her work at @Leah-Kohlenberg on Instagram.

COLUMBIA WHITE-TAILED DEER

[5]Heart & Hind, Twice Shy

Artist Leah Kohlenberg

---

[5] Hart & Hind are older English terms for a buck and doe of the Red Deer species once common in Great Britain.

CURIOUS ANIMALS

Autumn samaras spiral down in the air and tall grasses rise toward the sky,

COLUMBIA WHITE-TAILED DEER

within which you can catch a glimpse of the
bright-white ring around an eye

CURIOUS ANIMALS

of a Columbia White-tailed Deer!

COLUMBIA WHITE-TAILED DEER

With dun-colored hair and forward-facing
antler stem;

CURIOUS ANIMALS

its tail is fluffy long and held very tight
against its boxy square frame.

COLUMBIA WHITE-TAILED DEER

On islands down river, flood plains and marshes; they live at the margins of their own native land.

CURIOUS ANIMALS

No longer in their Willamette Valley woodlands,

COLUMBIA WHITE-TAILED DEER

they survive by our human backhand.

CURIOUS ANIMALS

Sporting small-sized heads on long slender necks,
these shy, hoofed ungulates emerge cautiously from the shrub.

COLUMBIA WHITE-TAILED DEER

White-ringed noses and curiously set ears
disappear at a breath.

CURIOUS ANIMALS

White fluffy tails raised like flags, moving like dogs as they run.

COLUMBIA WHITE-TAILED DEER

On the lower Columbia River morning fog has rolled in.

CURIOUS ANIMALS

More layers upon layers folding upon itself.
The dawn light has not yet hit the hilltops,

COLUMBIA WHITE-TAILED DEER

nor the deer bedded down in planted
woodlots,
dreaming of their dryer valley homeland.

CURIOUS ANIMALS

The Lower Columbia River is part of the Oregon Coast Range ecoregion. The "wet side" of the state has an abundance of riparian habitat, the interface between flowing waterways and land. It abounds with birds and mammals, aquatic and invertebrate species. Forage for the CWTD, deciduous trees and grasses, are planted in areas that historically flooded before dikes and levees were built.

Believed to have gone extinct by 1930, remnant populations of CWTD were discovered around 1967. Counted at 450 individuals, they were listed as endangered. These precious deer are heavily managed. Roosevelt Elk, who share the same habitat, are airlifted off the preserves meant solely for the CWTD. The ubiquitous Coyote is killed in order to allow fawns to survive.

Occasionally, select deer are moved between the two separate populations, ie lower Columbia River and Umpqua River, in order to diversify the genetics and keep these 1,200 animals strong (2020). Forty percent of the population live on refuges.

Learn to recognize their distinct features: The Hart's antlers, one stem with forward facing forks, the white eye and nose rings, the tail tucked, and they don't "stot" like other deer, ie hop or bound, they run like dogs.

*Permaculture principle #12 Creatively Use and Respond to Change. Over 100 years ago these deer relocated themselves to the margins of their preferred habitat. It could be said, that with this behavior, which includes eating different foods and bedding down in a different environment, that the CWTD did indeed creatively respond to change. Although there is little doubt that without heavy management[6], they likely would be one more line item on the extinction list.

---

[6] Most of these heavily managed deer, at least on one preserve, were observed to have a minimum of one ear tag. Some had both ears tagged, and a radio collar.

COLUMBIA WHITE-TAILED DEER

Artist **Anna Magruder** is a Portland, Oregon oil painter. Her favorite subjects are people and animals and whatever lies in between. Drifting between realism and surrealism, she loves recreating vintage America, re-imagining the lives and stories of the characters on her canvas or just exploring the emotional color of faces. View her work at www.AnnaMagruder.com.

WESTERN GRAY SQUIRREL

Sciurus griseus, A Haiku[7]

Artist Anna Magruder

---

[7] A small note about Haiku poetry, read them as 3 lines, facing pages. The syllables in a single Haiku are 5-7-5. They traditionally have little punctuation, have few prepositions and no extra words.

CURIOUS ANIMALS

Ponderosa life
Bundled needles counting three

WESTERN GRAY SQUIRREL

Sciurus griseus

CURIOUS ANIMALS

Hatted acorns stored

WESTERN GRAY SQUIRREL

Amongst Autumn Oak grove trees
Ground quick scampering

CURIOUS ANIMALS

Round covered nests domed
Hug thick trunks during Winter

WESTERN GRAY SQUIRREL

Curled tight against cold

CURIOUS ANIMALS

Foraging all Spring
Marbled truffles, fir seed, nuts

WESTERN GRAY SQUIRREL

Quick munch on catkins

CURIOUS ANIMALS

Summer heat cloaks round
Filtering down through green boughs

WESTERN GRAY SQUIRREL

Cool flat spray called 'drey'

CURIOUS ANIMALS

Canopy resting
On limbs hanging, belly stretched[8]

---

[8] This pose is often seen during hot temperatures and is referred to as "splooting"

WESTERN GRAY SQUIRREL

Aerial gloaming

CURIOUS ANIMALS

Encroaching sunrise
Diurnal mammal rises

WESTERN GRAY SQUIRREL

Once more, day begins

CURIOUS ANIMALS

On the southeast slopes of the Washington Cascades, the region is characterized by dry hills above waterways. Stands of Ponderosa Pine and Oregon White Oak tree bridge the dales in between. The Western Gray Squirrel nests in the conifer canopy and forages in both. Historically, they lived at lower elevations in the WA South Puget Trough through Columbia River Gorge and the East Cascades all the way to the Canada border. They were hunted vigorously for meat and fur. Thought to be on the verge of extinction, they have been found to live in three distinct breeding colonies in Washington State.

The WGS is usually quite avoidant of human activity and for those who don't know, could be mistaken for the opportunistic Eastern Gray Squirrel. However, WGS are the largest of the four native tree squirrels in the U.S.

West Coast region. It has a gray coat with white underbelly, bushy tail and white eye-rings.

Tree thinning, and other human practices have increased the hazards for WGS. Vehicular traffic, Coyote and Bobcat depredation appear to be the causes of the continued low population of this species. There is also some evidence that Wild Turkeys introduced to this region for hunting are in direct competition for food.

Currently in WA the WGS is listed as endangered. It is illegal to be hunted. In Oregon, they are identified as a sensitive species. This does not give a species as much consideration for protections as does an endangered listing.

CURIOUS ANIMALS

The WGS exhibits Permaculture Principle #7-Design from Patterns to Details. Here the WGS works within a large forest pattern of Oak and Pine. They prefer the tree canopy highway. So, seen from above, the aerial view of their habitat is another perspective from which we can discern how best to conserve the WGS population. In our own practices, we learn to design from something that is whole rather than taking it apart, or destroying it, *then* trying to discern how all the pieces work together.

WESTERN GRAY SQUIRREL

CURIOUS ANIMALS

AUTHOR BIO

Angela Dawn Goldsmith grew up among the forests, farms and cities of the Pacific Northwest. Her passion for natural systems has led her to become a certified permaculture teacher and Naturalist in Oregon. She applies these principles on her properties and volunteer designs/advises for other people and their land. Her extensive outdoor explorations have led her to deeper observations for how humans can be better partners in natural systems.

The *Curious Animals* series embodies her passion and knowledge with a love of tales that reach back to her childhood perched in trees, head deep in a book. You can learn more about Angela's projects, books and adventures at www.wildwoodviewgarden.wordpress.com.

www.ingramcontent.com/pod-product-compliance
Lightning Source LLC
Chambersburg PA
CBHW060509030426
42337CB00015B/1814